Renaissance Artists Who Inspired the World

 Written by Gregory Blanch and Roberta Stathis

Ballard & Tighe

Renaissance Artists
Who Inspired
the World

SERIES EDITOR: HEERA KANG
ART DIRECTOR: LILIANA CARTELLI
ILLUSTRATORS: PATRICIA DEWITT AND ROBIN DEWITT
EDITORIAL CONSULTANTS: PATRICE GOTSCH, JILL KINKADE
EDITORIAL STAFF: KRISTIN BELSHER, NINA CHUN,
ALLISON MANGRUM, SEAN O'BRIEN, SHERRY WICKS
SENIOR DESKTOP PUBLISHING COORDINATOR: KATHLEEN STYFFE
PRINTING COORDINATOR: CATHY SANCHEZ

An IDEA® Book by Ballard & Tighe, Publishers
P.O. Box 219, Brea, CA 92822-0219

ISBN #1-55501-593-X   Catalog #2-749

Contents

Introduction

Leonardo da Vinci and "Mona Lisa." Michelangelo and *David*. The names of these artists and their artwork may sound familiar to you. But what was the Renaissance all about? What is so special about the art and the artists from this time period?

The Renaissance was a time of rediscovery—finding new ways of doing and thinking about things. People during the Renaissance questioned ideas that had long been accepted as true, such as ideas about the church, the roles of men and women, and politics and government. It was a great time for new ideas, especially in art.

This book gives you a glimpse of five important Renaissance artists from Italy—Sandro Botticelli, Leonardo da Vinci, Michelangelo, Raphael, and Sofonisba Anguissola. Each is remembered for different reasons, but all of them made a mark in art history for creating breathtaking art like no one had done before.

The Renaissance celebrated creativity and different ways of doing things and thinking. This book is devoted to inspiring the Renaissance spirit in all who read it.

SANDRO BOTTICELLI
c. 1444-1510
Famous Works: "The Birth of Venus,"
"Primavera," "Adoration of the Magi,"
"Madonna of the Magnificent,"
"Madonna of the Pomegranate"

FRANCE

PORTUGAL

SPAIN

LEONARDO DA VINCI
1452-1519
Famous Works: "The Last Supper,"
"Annunciation," "Mona Lisa"

MICHELANGELO
1475-1564
Famous Works: *David*,
Ceiling of Sistine Chapel, *Pieta*

GERMANY

SWITZERLAND   AUSTRIA

ITALY

Mediterranean Sea

RAPHAEL
1483-1520
Famous Works: "Sposalizio"
(Marriage of the Virgin), "Disputa"
(Disputation Concerning the Holy
Sacrament), "Sistine Madonna"

SOFONISBA ANGUISSOLA
c. 1532-1625
Famous Works: "Portrait of the Artist's
Sister Minerva," "Self Portrait,"
"The Chess Game"

Time Line

Having a common system to date events helps us compare events occurring at the same time in different parts of the world. Many experts in the Western world use the B.C./A.D. dating system. This system dates events from the birth of Jesus Christ, a central figure in the Christian religion. Events that took place before his birth are referred to as "before Christ" or B.C. dates. Traditionally, the term B.C. begins to be used around the time when human beings began to lead a more settled life, about 11,000 years ago. A.D. stands for the Latin words *anno Domini*, which means "in the year of the Lord." A.D. dates are given to events that occurred after Jesus's birth. A growing number of historians, archaeologists, and other academics also use the terms B.C.E. and C.E. to refer to these same periods of time. B.C.E. stands for "before Christian era" or "before common era." C.E. refers to "Christian era" or "common era." Some academic experts even use the term B.P., which stands for "before present." When we are not exactly sure of the date of an event, we use the Latin word *circa* which means "about." *Circa* is abbreviated c.

c. 1350 — The Renaissance begins

c. 1483 — Sandro Botticelli creates "The Birth of Venus"

A.D. **1300**

c. 1450s — Johannes Gutenberg develops his printing press

TIPS on Reading a Time Line

Find the beginning and end dates.

Look at the far left and far right sides of the time line. These dates show you the range of time you are focusing on. What is the range of time for this book?

Check if the time line includes both B.C. and A.D. dates.

This book focuses on A.D. dates. When you read a time line with B.C. dates, remember that starting from the left, the B.C. dates become lower until the "0." After that, the A.D. dates go higher.

Think of other events that happened around the same time.

In the time line below, you can see that all of the artists in this book lived around the same period of time. As you read about the artists, think about how their experiences were the same and different.

Jump in!

Copy the time line onto a sheet of paper, but make the end date on the far right side extend to the present day. Insert yourself into the time line to see how long ago the events in this book happened. You also can include other important dates you have learned about.

c. 1495-1498 — Leonardo da Vinci paints "The Last Supper"

c. 1508 — Raphael goes to Rome to paint the Sistine Chapel

c. 1600 — The Renaissance ends

A.D. 1650

c. 1560 — Sofonisba Anguissola paints pictures of the Spanish royal family

c. 1496-1501 — Michelangelo sculpts the *Pieta*

The Renaissance

Europe was an exciting place to live during the period from about 1350 to 1600. Major cultural, religious, and scientific changes were taking place in European society. These changes began in Italy and soon spread throughout Europe. Eventually, the changes affected the entire world.

Historians have given names to large periods of time in European history. They call the time of the ancient Romans and Greeks the "ancient world" or the "classical world." They refer to the period after the fall of Rome (A.D. 476) until about 1350 as the "Middle Ages." Toward the end of the Middle Ages, people began to look more critically at church teachings and ideas about politics, religion, and education. They were interested in learning about the ideas of the ancient Romans and Greeks. They wanted to understand the art and architecture that the ancient Greeks and Romans had created—this was art and architecture that Italians saw around them every day. Some people thought it was as if society was being reborn. This "rebirth" started in Italy, but eventually spread throughout Europe. Historians call this period of European history—the time from about 1350 to 1600—the Renaissance.

Florence, Italy was the center of Renaissance art. This photograph shows the city of Florence today. The dome you see on the city's cathedral was built during the Renaissance.

The First Renaissance Man

Many people call Francesco Petrarch the "father of the **Renaissance**." He was born in 1304 in Arezzo, Italy, and became known as one of the greatest writers of the Italian Renaissance. Petrarch thought he was living in a new age of rediscovery. He believed human beings could make choices in their lives, ask questions, and learn new ideas. Throughout his life, he put great emphasis on education. He wrote, "I cannot get enough books. It may be that I have already more than I need, but … books … have a special charm. … Books delight us through and through, they talk with us, they give us good counsel, they enter into a living and intimate companionship with us." Petrarch collected many books about the ideas of ancient Greeks and Romans.

As scholars and artists studied the ideas and art of the ancient Greeks and Romans, they became less willing to accept an idea simply because the church or some other authority said it was true. They wanted to discover things for themselves and create their own ideas.

Look to the Source

Petrarch was very interested in learning. He liked to write. He also liked to collect and read books. Petrarch thought people of his time were entering a new age of rediscovery and learning. In the paragraph below, you can read what Petrarch wrote about the importance of books in his life.

"I cannot get enough books. It may be that I have already more than I need, but it is with books as it is with other things: success in acquisition spurs the desire to get still more. Books, indeed, have a special charm. Gold, silver, gems, … a house of marble, a well-tilled field, paintings, a steed with splendid trappings—things such as these give a silent and superficial pleasure. Books delight us through and through, they talk with us, they give us good counsel, they enter into a living and intimate companionship with us."

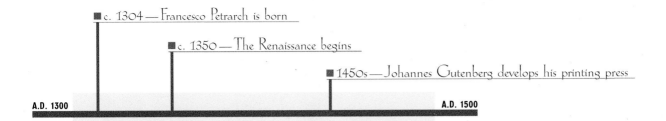

- c. 1304 — Francesco Petrarch is born
- c. 1350 — The Renaissance begins
- 1450s — Johannes Gutenberg develops his printing press

A.D. 1300 — A.D. 1500

These scholars and artists did not reject the church or their Christian faith; however, they began to have a more **secular** view of the world. They began to be more concerned with human achievements and interests. This way of thinking is called **humanism**. Humanists thought the individual's power and dignity were most important. Humanists argued that people could improve themselves through education. They believed there were no limits to what an individual could achieve. Humanists thought people should have knowledge in many areas and develop many interests and talents. A person who achieved this ideal was called a "Renaissance man."

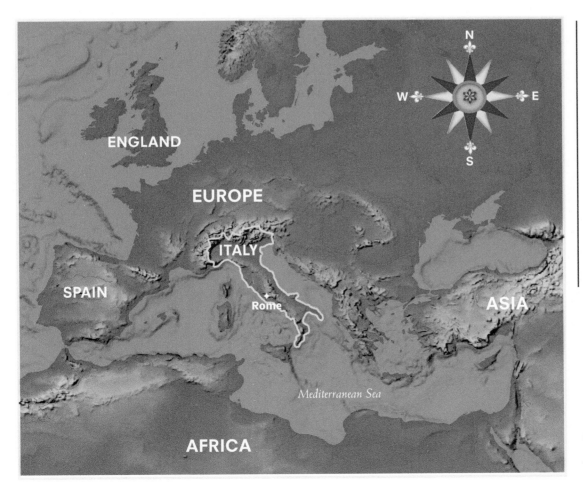

humanism: a way of thinking that is concerned with human achievement and a belief in the importance of individual power, dignity, and the ability to improve through education

secular: not specifically related to religion or to a religious body

Renaissance ideas began in Italy and later spread throughout Europe.

11

Lorenzo di Medici supported important Renaissance artists. One artist, Benozzo Gozzoli (1420-1497), painted "The Procession of the Magi," which includes this portrayal of Lorenzo di Medici.

Renaissance Society

Italy during the Renaissance was made up of about 250 independent city-states. Some were small and others were large. Each city-state collected taxes, defended its territory, and made and enforced its own laws. Many Italian city-states were **republics** governed by an elected group of people. However, individual **tyrants** or groups of rich families ruled most Italian city-states. They ran the governments of the city-states so that their businesses would make money. Some of the most important Italian city-states were Florence, Venice, Milan, Genoa, and Siena. The city-states competed with one another for power and prestige.

republic: a form of government where people choose their leaders

patron: a person who supports, protects, or champions something

tyrant: a ruler who uses power in a harsh, cruel way

Italian cities were busy places during the Renaissance. The streets were filled with merchants, people shopping, farmers, priests and nuns, visiting scholars, and artists. Buildings in towns were usually two- or three-stories high. Shops were on the first floor so customers could look in the windows to see what was for sale. Shopkeepers lived on the upper floors. Everyone threw their garbage out the windows. No one picked up after the horses, oxen, and pigs that wandered the streets. Imagine the noise and the smell!

Most people in these city-states were part of the lower class. About 20-25% of the people were part of the upper class. The richest and most powerful members of the upper class in each city-state controlled the government. Some of these rich and powerful people used their wealth to support the new ideas of the Renaissance. Lorenzo di Medici, for example, became one of Florence's most important **patrons**. He began a school for promising young artists, including Michelangelo. Lorenzo di Medici also supported and encouraged another important artist, Leonardo da Vinci. Patrons from other city-states competed with Florence for artists. Each city-state wanted to have the most beautiful buildings and artwork. The Roman Catholic Church also played an important role in competing for Renaissance artists. The churches in each community wanted artists to beautify their buildings. This strong competition for artwork had an important effect on the role of artists in society.

The Renaissance Spreads

By 1475, the ideas of the Italian Renaissance had spread to northern Europe. One way people learned about these ideas was by way of books. During the Middle Ages, books were written by hand on parchment or vellum, both of which came from animal hides. With the introduction of paper-making technology in Europe, wood pulp and other plant materials could be used to make paper. This meant that books were much less costly to make. In the 1450s, another important technological advancement took place. Johannes Gutenberg, a German goldsmith, developed the printing press. The first book Gutenberg printed was the Bible. Soon, however, ancient Greek and Roman texts, as well as works by Renaissance scholars, were being printed and sold throughout Europe.

In the 1450s, Johannes Gutenberg developed a printing press that could print books much faster than before. The printing of books helped ideas spread throughout Europe and around the world. This picture shows Gutenberg examining a printed page.

By 1500, about 1,000 European printers had published more than nine million books. People could buy books on many subjects in different languages. For the first time, many people could read the Bible because it had been translated into German, French, and other languages. Governments used flyers and small booklets to announce wars, treaties, and reports of battles. More people learned to read. They learned about new ideas and about new ways of understanding the world.

apprentice: a person who goes to work for another person; in return for this work, the apprentice learns a trade, art, or business

guild: an organization of people of the same trade or interests; people form guilds for protection, to maintain standards, or for other purposes

mason: a person who builds or works with stone or brick

The Changing Role of Artists during the Renaissance

Today, we think of Sandro Botticelli, Leonardo da Vinci, Michelangelo, Raphael, and Sofonisba Anguissola as geniuses. Museums and private art collectors are willing to pay millions of dollars for their artwork. Before the Renaissance, however, people who painted, sculpted, and created other artistic work were considered in the same category as carpenters and **masons**. They began as **apprentices** and learned their skills from **guild** masters. Guild masters were highly skilled artisans, but they were just craft workers nonetheless. During the Renaissance, however, this view of artists began to change. People began to appreciate and admire an artist's individual style, skill, imagination, and intelligence. Artists became famous for their work. And, as patrons competed for their skills, many artists also became very wealthy.

Today, we honor great artists, such as Leonardo da Vinci. However, before the Renaissance, artists were considered skilled laborers. This statue of da Vinci stands in Florence, Italy.

15

Michelangelo's sculpture, *Pieta*, is an example of how Renaissance artists showed strong religious feelings in their work. *Pieta* is an Italian word for "pity." A pieta is a painting or sculpture of the Virgin Mary holding her dead son, Jesus.

The Power of Art to Convey Ideas

Renaissance artists created thousands of works that show strong religious feelings. In this way, they continued the tradition of artists who lived and worked during the Middle Ages. As in the Middle Ages, art in the Renaissance helped people express their faith. Renaissance artists painted pictures and created sculptures of scenes and people from the Bible. However, they also focused on nonreligious or secular themes. Renaissance art showed the power and beauty of human beings. It showed feeling, movement, and life. Renaissance artists painted pictures and sculpted figures of ancient Roman and Greek gods. They painted realistic portraits of patrons. They even included pictures of themselves in their artwork.

Renaissance artists used color, shading, **perspective**, and scientific knowledge to create accurate pictures of people, animals, plants, buildings, and landscapes. Men such as Leonardo da Vinci and Michelangelo even **dissected** dead bodies in order to learn more about human **anatomy**. Renaissance artists experimented with new materials, including oil paints, and new surfaces, including ceilings! They created sculptures "in the round." Such sculptures stood up on their own and allowed the viewer to look at them from any point of view. This was different from sculpture in the Middle Ages, which usually was carved into a wall or panel.

During the Middle Ages, almost all art was created for the glory of God. Renaissance artists created artwork with religious themes, too, but their artwork also began to focus on human beings—their feelings, experiences, and form. Their art reflected advances in science, mathematics, engineering, understanding of human anatomy, and interest in human experiences and individuals. The new emphasis on humanism had a profound impact on European society and helped to usher in cultural, religious, and scientific changes that ultimately affected and involved the entire world.

anatomy: the structure of an animal or plant, or of any of its parts

dissect: to cut apart, especially for study

perspective: a technique (based on mathematical principles) of making some objects look closer and others appear farther away

Quick Quiz

1. Who is referred to as the "father of the Renaissance"?

2. How did Renaissance ideas spread throughout Europe?

3. How was art during this period different from what had been created before?

Sandro Botticelli
Expressing Emotion through Art

"Sandro Botticelli" was not the name his parents gave him. The baby boy born around 1444 or 1445 in Florence was called Alessandro (Sandro) di Mariano Filipepi. How did he get the name Botticelli? One story says that his older brother, who was very big, was called "Botticella." In Italian *botticella* means "keg," which is a large barrel. It is said that Sandro was given the nickname "Botticelli," which means "little barrel." This nickname stuck. Today, Sandro Botticelli—the "little barrel"—is considered one of the greatest painters of the Italian Renaissance.

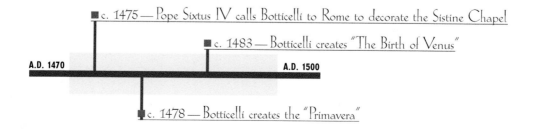

c. 1475 — Pope Sixtus IV calls Botticelli to Rome to decorate the Sistine Chapel

c. 1483 — Botticelli creates "The Birth of Venus"

A.D. 1470   A.D. 1500

c. 1478 — Botticelli creates the "Primavera"

Sandro Botticelli created many paintings that show Mary and the baby Jesus, but his most famous works reflect secular themes.

Fast Facts

GIVEN NAME: Alessandro di Mariano Filipepi
BORN: c. 1444; Florence, Italy
DIED: 1510; Florence, Italy
LIVED: Florence (two years in Rome, c. 1481-82)
FAMILY: Father, Mariano Filipepi; brother, Francesco
FAMOUS WORKS: "The Birth of Venus," "Primavera," "Adoration of the Magi," "Madonna of the Magnificent," "Madonna of the Pomegranate"

A Talented Young Artist

As a young boy, Sandro found no pleasure in studying the traditional subjects students learned at school. He wanted to paint and create art! His father was a tanner and by tradition Sandro's job should have been to make leather like his father. However, Sandro's talent as an artist was recognized at an early age, and his father sent him to be the apprentice of a local painter and goldsmith. Sandro quickly learned all he could from his first art teacher. His next teacher was Filipo Lippi, a famous painter. Under Lippi's influence, Sandro learned how to create "panels." Panels are outlines that guide an artist when he or she begins a painting. In his early years, several other artists also influenced Sandro Botticelli. One in particular was Andrea del Verrocchio. In addition to Sandro Botticelli, Verrocchio worked with other famous Renaissance artists, including Leonardo da Vinci who you will read about in the next chapter. Verrocchio taught Sandro how to use color to show great emotion in his paintings. For example, Sandro learned how to use soft pastels to show a character's feelings. Some of his first paintings were so good that the Goldsmith Guild of Florence appointed Botticelli to paint the "Coronation of the Virgin" in honor of the guild's patron saint. By the time he was 24, Botticelli started his own artist's workshop.

commission: to place an order for

modest: have a shy or reserved manner; quiet and humble

By most accounts, Botticelli was a **modest** person. He did not enjoy a lavish or wealthy lifestyle. Actually, money did not seem to be very important to him. He was fortunate to live during the time that the Medici family ruled Florence. This was important to artists like Botticelli because members of the Medici family as well as other wealthy Florentine families were great patrons of the arts. They **commissioned** works of art and provided support for painters, sculptors, and architects, as well as writers and scholars.

20

Botticelli Makes Powerful Friends

Over many years, Botticelli painted several portraits of various Medici family members. Around 1473-1475, he painted the "Adoration of the Magi," which shows the Biblical scene of the three wise men honoring the baby Jesus. Botticelli used several members of the Medici family as models for some of the figures in this painting. In fact, Botticelli himself appears in the right-hand side of the painting. He is shown wearing a yellow **cloak**.

Around 1475, Pope Sixtus IV had an old church in the **Vatican** torn down and built a small church in its place. He named the new building after himself—it was called the Sistine **Chapel**. The pope invited many of the most famous artists of the time to use their talents in decorating the interior of the chapel. One of these artists was Sandro Botticelli. In all, Botticelli created three paintings in the interior of the chapel.

chapel: a small church

cloak: a loose outer garment without sleeves; like a cape

St. Peter's Basilica: a Christian church named after Peter, one of Jesus's 12 followers; after his death, Peter was named a saint (abbreviation is St.) for having lived a holy life

Vatican: the official residence (or home) of the pope; the Vatican is located in Vatican City, an independent state located within the city of Rome

The pope was overjoyed with Botticelli's contribution to the decoration of the Sistine Chapel. This is a view of St. Peter's Square. The Sistine Chapel is to the right of the dome of **St. Peter's Basilica**.

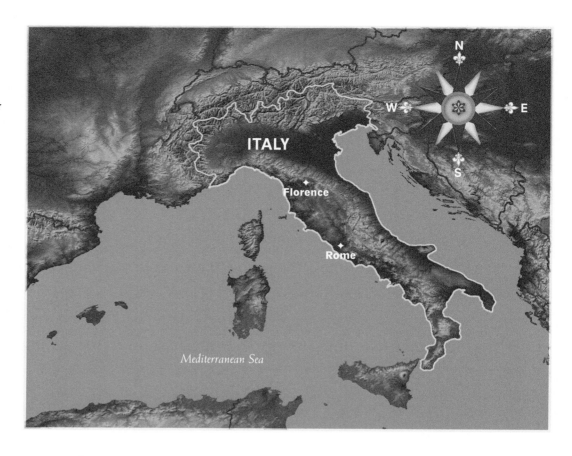

Sandro Botticelli lived most of his life in Florence. He traveled to Rome to paint the interior of a new church called the Sistine Chapel.

biography: a written account of a person's life; a life history

fresco: an artwork created by painting on damp plaster with watercolor paints

Sandro's three pieces in the Sistine Chapel were a special kind of painting called **fresco**. His frescoes showed scenes from the Old and New Testaments of the Bible. Pope Sixtus IV was overjoyed with Botticelli's creative contribution to the decoration of the Sistine Chapel. A famous **biography** of Botticelli by Giorgio Vasari said Botticelli was highly praised for these works and "received from the Pope a good sum of money... ." After he completed his work at the Vatican, Botticelli went home to Florence.

Botticelli's Most Famous Paintings

Botticelli returned to Florence and to his very busy workshop. During the next few years, he created several paintings, which some art historians say are his best works. Two of these works, "Primavera" (c. 1478) and "The Birth of Venus" (c. 1483) are his most famous.

This is a close-up of the painting, "The Birth of Venus." It shows the birth of the ancient Roman goddess of love, Venus. This painting is an example of one of Botticelli's secular works. Even today, tens of thousands of people wait in long lines to see these paintings at the Uffizi Gallery in Florence, Italy.

The artistic style of these paintings is very different from the style of other artists of the time. You can see this in the way Botticelli used color and the slender form of his figures.

Botticelli especially enjoyed creating art that had a **literary** theme. In the 1490s, Botticelli took on an ambitious project. He created a series of drawings to illustrate Dante's *The Divine Comedy*. These drawings are housed in the Vatican Museums. Botticelli also painted several pictures inspired by the writing of Boccacio, a famous author of the late Middle Ages.

literary: relating to literature (written works)

Bonfire of the Vanities

bonfire of the vanities: a large outdoor fire in which items that are not considered "useful" or worthwhile are burned

Fra: brother; a title given to an Italian friar or monk; abbreviation of the Italian word *frate*

During the later 1490s, Florence underwent much upheaval. The Medici family was expelled from the city. About 1498, a Dominican monk, **Fra Girolamo Savonarola**, began to speak publicly against anything that wasn't necessary for the life of man. He was a powerful speaker and convinced many people to agree with his view. Many young men and women marched from house to house in Florence urging people to bring to the city center their fancy clothes, jewelry, paintings, and other works of art. All of these "worldly possessions" were piled high and then set on fire. They were completely destroyed in what came to be known as a **"bonfire of the vanities."** For a period of time, Botticelli became a very devoted follower of Savonarola. His work during this time reflects a stronger Christian theme.

Botticelli's Art Survives

During the last few years of his life, Botticelli depended on patrons and friends for financial support. When he died in 1510, almost no one was interested in his paintings. The work of this "little barrel" who is so famous and admired today was virtually ignored for almost 300 years. The first group of people who "rediscovered" Botticelli were British artists living in Italy during the late 1800s. Today, his work is on display in galleries in Europe and the United States, and he is considered one of the greatest artists of the Renaissance.

Quick Quiz

1. How did Sandro Botticelli get his name?
2. Describe the educational process Botticelli followed in order to become an artist.
3. How do you think Botticelli's patrons influenced the themes in his art?
4. Do you think Botticelli was a "Renaissance man"? Explain your answer.

Look to the Source

Throughout his life, Sandro Botticelli was a man who did not want to be disturbed while he was trying to create his art. His biographer, Giorgio Vasari, tells the following story:

"A weaver set up eight noisy, clattering looms in the house next to Sandro's. The painter could not work; he could not even stay at home. When he asked for an end of the disturbance, the reply was that the weaver both could and would do as he liked in his own house. Sandro then balanced an enormous weight of stone on the roof of his house that was higher than his neighbor's. The stone threatened to fall when the wall was shaken, and had it done so it would have crushed the weaver's roof, floors, looms, and workmen. The man hastened to Sandro in terror, but got the same reply he himself had given: that Sandro both could and would do as he liked in his own house. Thereafter the weaver became a less troublesome neighbor."

A book written around A.D. 77, *Natural History*, inspired Renaissance painters such as Sandro Botticelli. In *Natural History*, the ancient Roman writer, Pliny the Elder, described artistic techniques and famous paintings of ancient Rome. For example, Pliny described fresco painting, which became one of the most important painting techniques in the Renaissance.

Leonardo da Vinci
Artist, Inventor, and Thinker

eonardo da Vinci is one of the greatest artists, inventors, and thinkers who ever lived. He was born on April 15, 1452 in the small town of Vinci, about 20 miles from Florence. Just like Sandro Botticelli, Leonardo was born in an exciting time in art history. And he was born in the area where the Renaissance began. Leonardo's father was a leading citizen of the community of Vinci. He was responsible for preparing legal documents.

You might think that Leonardo was a very lucky boy to have such advantages. However, he faced problems, too. His mother was only a peasant girl, and she was not married to his father. During that time, there were strict rules for children whose parents were not married. For example, they could not go to the university. Nor could they become doctors or lawyers or bankers. However, Leonardo had great talents. People said he could sing beautifully, but his greatest skill seemed to be drawing.

Young Leonardo became an apprentice to Andrea del Verrocchio. Among other things, Leonardo learned to make paints and paint brushes.

pigment: any substance used as coloring; pigments are usually mixed with water, oil, or another base to produce paint

The Art of Becoming an Artist

When he was about 11 or 12 years old, Leonardo's father took him from the little country town where he was born to the city of Florence. Leonardo became an apprentice to a famous artist named Andrea del Verrocchio. At first, Leonardo ran errands, swept the floor, and did other small jobs around the artist's workshop. Later, he learned to make brushes and mix **pigments** to make colors. He practiced drawing and helped with the paintings and sculptures Verrocchio was making.

When he was about 20, Leonardo joined the painters' guild in Florence. He worked in Florence for 10 years. When he was 30, Leonardo decided to go north to Milan. Leonardo sent a letter to the powerful ruler of Milan, Duke Ludovico Sforza, asking for work. In the letter, he did not focus on his artistic skills. Instead, he wrote mostly about his ideas for "machines of war" and about architecture.

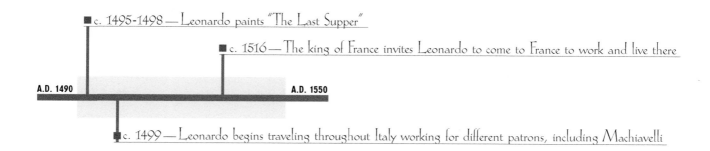

c. 1495-1498 — Leonardo paints "The Last Supper"

c. 1516 — The king of France invites Leonardo to come to France to work and live there

A.D. 1490   A.D. 1550

c. 1499 — Leonardo begins traveling throughout Italy working for different patrons, including Machiavelli

Leonardo Breaks from Tradition

monk: a man who pursues a life of religious service

The duke did not answer Leonardo's letter—at least not right away. So Leonardo began to paint a picture for a local church. The **monks** who hired him were clear about the kind of picture they wanted. They said it should be very traditional, like all the pictures they had ever seen. But Leonardo had other ideas. He painted people in the picture who looked like real people. They were not stiff and serious figures. The monks and others were surprised at this new way of painting, but many admired his work. One of the admirers was the duke, who decided to become Leonardo's patron.

Leonardo stayed in Milan and worked for the duke until 1499. Duke Sforza asked him to take on many challenging projects. Leonardo designed costumes, thought of a way to heat bath water, designed new weapons, and painted pictures of important people and other subjects.

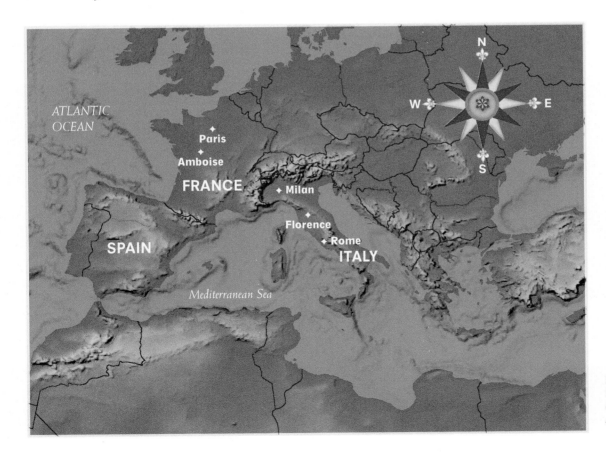

Leonardo da Vinci lived in Florence, Milan, Rome, and in the French city of Amboise.

The Last Supper Experiment

One of the most famous pictures Leonardo painted during this time is called "The Last Supper." The duke wanted a picture painted for a local church in Milan. Leonardo decided to paint the picture on a wall in the room where the monks ate. "The Last Supper" shows Jesus and his followers at dinner the night before Jesus was put to death. The way Leonardo painted the picture almost made it seem as if Jesus and his followers were eating with the monks!

This painting reveals Leonardo da Vinci's knowledge of science and mathematics. It is apparent in the skillful way he shows perspective. You have the feeling of space and depth behind the people seated at the table. Leonardo da Vinci, like other Renaissance artists, believed the artist must know the rules of perspective as well as the laws of nature, including an understanding of human anatomy. Leonardo experimented with a new way of painting for this picture. Unfortunately, his experiment was not a success. The paint started to chip off almost right away. Still, many people say it is one of the most beautiful paintings in the world.

Leonardo's "The Last Supper" shows Jesus and his followers at dinner the night before Jesus was put to death.

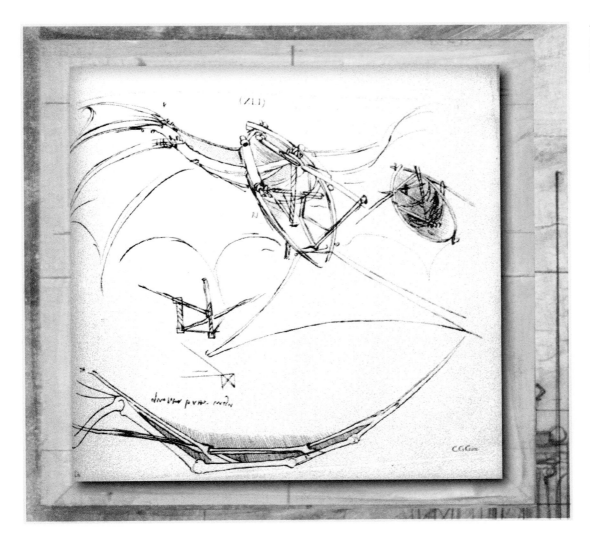

Leonardo's Notebooks

Leonardo wrote pages and pages of notes about his work and about the things he saw around him. He wrote notes about what he learned about the human body. He wrote notes about experiments he **conducted**. He also wrote notes about his inventions, including such things as a flying machine. Of course, he drew pictures to illustrate many of these ideas. He wrote his notes backwards, which led some to think that he was trying to keep others from stealing his ideas. Sometimes he wrote his notes in code, which was much more effective in keeping his secrets.

conduct: to direct or control

Look to the Source

Much of what we know about Leonardo comes from the book written by Giorgio Vasari, *The Lives of the Artists*. The excerpt below is from Vasari's introduction to the chapter on Leonardo da Vinci. Vasari described Leonardo as a genius.

" ... Sometimes ... a single body is lavishly supplied with such beauty, grace, and ability that wherever the individual turns, each of his actions is so divine that he leaves behind all other men and clearly makes himself known as a genius endowed by God ... . Men saw this in Leonardo da Vinci."

In 1483, Leonardo designed the first parachute. Leonardo's parachute had poles running from the top to the bottom. Of course, it was very rigid. More than 500 years later, a man tested Leonardo's design by using it to skydive. It worked! Leonardo wrote in his notes about the design:

"If a man had a tent made of line, of which all the **apertures** have been stopped up, and it be twelve **braccia** (21 feet) across and twelve feet in depth, he will be able to throw himself down from any great height without sustaining any injury."

aperture: a hole or gap

braccia: a unit of measurement equal to about 1.75 feet

Leonardo met other Renaissance masters during his travels around Italy.
They included artist Michelangelo (left) and philosopher Machiavelli (right).

Meeting Other Renaissance Masters

Leonardo's years in Milan ended in 1499 when French soldiers attacked and took the duke prisoner. Leonardo traveled all over Italy for the next 16 years working for different patrons. One of the people he met during this time was Niccolo Machiavelli, a **diplomat** from Florence. Machiavelli helped Leonardo get work in Florence. Leonardo was asked to paint a battle scene in a government building. A young artist, Michelangelo, was asked to paint a second picture in the same building. Leonardo and Michelangelo did not like each other very much. They often argued and insulted each another. In the end, for different reasons, neither man finished his painting.

diplomat: a person who represents a government in relations with other governments

About 1516, the king of France invited Leonardo to work for him. He took one of his most famous paintings with him. It was called the "Mona Lisa."

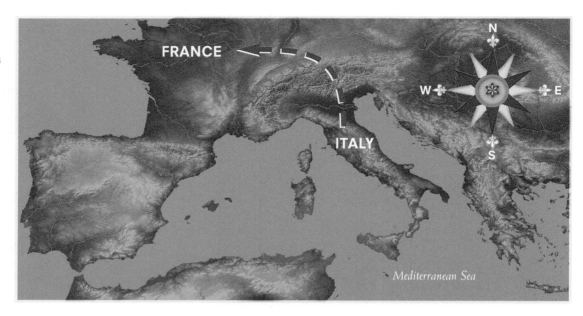

To France!

After he left Milan, Leonardo faced many problems. After his father and uncle died, the family fought about who would get their money. In the end, Leonardo did not get anything because his father and mother had never married. Leonardo also was getting old and was often sick. He had never married and did not have a family to take care of him. Then, around 1516, something wonderful happened. The king of France invited Leonardo to come to France. The king promised to give him a place to live and good pay. Leonardo agreed happily and set out for France. He took his notebooks and several paintings along with him. One of these paintings is probably the most famous painting in the world. It is a picture of a woman smiling. If you guessed the "Mona Lisa," you are correct! This painting now hangs in the Louvre, one of the most important museums in France and in the world.

Leonardo lived as the king's honored guest until he died at the age of 67 on May 2, 1519. Today when people hear the name "Leonardo da Vinci," they remember one of the greatest artists, inventors, and thinkers of all time.

Quick Quiz

1. Many famous artists of Leonardo's time began as apprentices to the same man. Who was this man?

2. How did Leonardo keep people from stealing his ideas?

3. What advantages did Leonardo have in life? What obstacles?

4. When Leonardo sent a letter asking for a job from the duke of Milan, why do you think Leonardo wrote mostly about his ideas for "machines of war"?

Leonardo's "Mona Lisa" shows a woman with a curious smile. This painting hangs in the Louvre, a museum in France (shown below).

Michelangelo
"Many Kings, but Only One Michelangelo"

The small boy stood on the dusty street and looked into the workshop. He was late going home and his father would be angry that he stopped—especially at this doorway. His father was paying a tutor to teach him Latin and Greek. His father always reminded him to learn the "words that will help you get a good job." Whenever the boy said he was more interested in drawing, his father had become very, very angry. His father said the family did not have money for such foolishness. The boy's job was to "learn those things that will bring honor to the family name." Nonetheless, the boy had stopped to look through the window of the workshop ...

At first, none of the artisans inside noticed the boy. As each minute passed, however, he moved closer to the door. Finally, he was inside. As he entered the large room, a few of the younger boys quickly looked at him. The boy knew they were about his same age, but they acted as if they were much more important. But the boy didn't care what they thought of him. He saw their work, and he knew he was better—much better.

When Michelangelo was about 13 years old, he became an apprentice in a well-known Florentine painter's workshop.

GIVEN NAME: Michelangelo Buonarroti
BORN: March 1475; Caprese, Tuscany
DIED: February 1564; Rome
LIVED: Florence; Rome
FAMILY: Father, Ludovico; mother, Francesca Neri
FAMOUS WORKS: *David*, Ceiling of Sistine Chapel, *Pieta*

Fast Facts

Michelangelo realized that the noisy workshop had suddenly become very quiet. And in the next moment, he heard the deep voice of the master of the workshop coming from behind him. "Who is this boy and why is he here bothering us? Get out!" The boy was scared and turned toward the voice. He stood before Florence's greatest artist. The boy tried to speak, but no words came out. The man standing before him became impatient. Finally, the boy said, "Master Ghirlandaio, I am Buonarroti."

"Do you know me?" asked Ghirlandaio. "Yes, of course you know me. I am an important artist."

"Yes, sir. I have looked closely at your work," said Michelangelo.

"But why are you here, Buonarroti? You waste our valuable time!"

The boy was afraid, but he knew he would be better than any of the apprentices. He turned to the man and said, "I am Michelangelo Buonarroti ... and I can draw." The man was surprised that the boy would speak so boldly. Who did this young child think he was? He smiled a little, and then said, "Well Buonarroti, let us see how good you are ..."

struggle: to make a strong effort to solve a problem

The story of the boy in the artist's workshop is a fictional account based on facts we know about Michelangelo's early life. Michelangelo Buonarroti was born in a small village near Florence, Italy in 1475. He was born during the Renaissance—one of the greatest periods of artistic accomplishment in the history of the Western world. During his early life, he **struggled** to convince his father that he wanted to be an artist. When he was about 13 years old, he became an apprentice with Ghirlandaio, a well-known Florentine painter. He didn't remain an apprentice for long. Ghirlandaio quickly recognized Michelangelo's talent for drawing and painting. But Michelangelo's true love was sculpture.

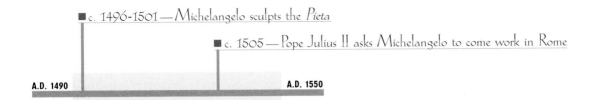
An Invitation from Lorenzo di Medici

Lorenzo di Medici, the most important leader in Florence, invited Michelangelo to study sculpture. Lorenzo di Medici became Michelangelo's patron. For the next four years, Michelangelo spent almost all of his time learning the art of sculpture. During this time, he began to study the human body. This helped him make sculptures that looked like real people. By the time he was 16 years old, Michelangelo had created two important sculptures. However, when Lorenzo di Medici died, Michelangelo no longer had his patron's support.

During the next few years, Michelangelo traveled to other Italian city-states such as Bologna and Rome. He was looking for new patrons to support his work. In Rome, he carved two more sculptures in the years between 1496 and 1501. One of these sculptures, the *Pieta*, is one of his most famous works. Michelangelo was only about 25 or 30 years old when he created the *Pieta*. It still stands today in St. Peter's Basilica in Rome.

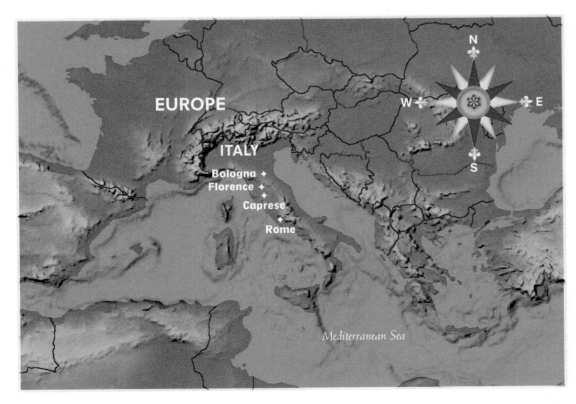

Artists during the Renaissance needed rich patrons to support their work. After Lorenzo di Medici died, Michelangelo traveled to Italian city-states such as Bologna and Rome looking for new patrons.

Florence and David

When he finished these works, Michelangelo went home to Florence. People knew of the work he had done in Rome. Michelangelo wrote in his diary, "When I returned to Florence, I found myself famous." The leaders of the city asked him to carve a statue. Michelangelo was excited about this work. He wrote in his diary, "I locked myself away in a workshop behind the cathedral, hammered and **chiseled** at the towering block for three long years." He took a huge piece of **marble** and carved the figure of David. David is the boy in the Bible who fought with only a **slingshot** against the larger and stronger Goliath. Some people say it is the most beautiful statue ever created. It was placed in the center of Florence as a symbol of the republic. Michelangelo wrote, "Archways were torn down, narrow streets were widened … it took forty men five days to move it. Once in place, all Florence was astounded."

Michelangelo carved his *David* from a huge piece of marble. Today, the statue stands in the Galleria dell' Accademia in Florence.

40

The Sistine Ceiling and St. Peter's Basilica

In 1505, after Michelangelo finished the statue of David, Pope Julius II asked him to come to Rome. The pope and Michelangelo had a difficult relationship. Despite their problems, however, Michelangelo completed several of his greatest works in Rome, including the frescoes on the ceiling of the Sistine Chapel. During this last part of his life, Michelangelo also designed buildings. He was asked to be the chief architect of Rome's St. Peter's Basilica. When he finished this work, he went back to the sculpting that he loved so much. In his final days, he spent most of his time alone. He worked with his chisels and his pieces of marble. He died in 1564 when he was 88 years old. One person said, "The world has many kings, but only one Michelangelo."

This is a self-portrait by Michelangelo.

Look to the Source

Here is an excerpt from a letter Michelangelo, who was 21 years old, wrote to Lorenzo di Medici in 1496:

"Christ. On the 2nd day of July 1496

Magnificent Lorenzo, etc. – This is only to let you know that we arrived safely last Saturday and at once went to call upon the Cardinal di San Giorgio, to whom I presented your letter. He seemed pleased to see me and immediately desired me to go and look at certain figures; this took me all day, so I could not deliver your other letters that day. Then on Sunday, having gone to his new house, the Cardinal sent for me. I waited upon him, and he asked me what I thought of the things I had seen. In reply to this I told him what I thought; and I certainly think he has many beautiful things. Then the Cardinal asked me whether I had courage enough to attempt some work of art of my own. I replied that I could not do anything as fine, but that he should see what I could do. We have bought a piece of marble for a life-sized figure and on Monday I shall begin work … ."

After he finished painting the ceiling of the Sistine Chapel, Michelangelo returned to Florence. This work took many years and placed a great physical burden on Michelangelo. Later he wrote the following in his diary:

"After four tortured years, more than 400 over life-sized figures, I felt as old and weary as Jeremiah [a Biblical figure who lived to a very old age]. I was only 37, yet friends did not recognize the old man I had become."

Quick Quiz

1. What is the name of the famous sculpture Michelangelo completed before he was 30 years old?

2. Michelangelo completed a very large statue entitled *David*, one of the most famous statues in the world. Who was David? What is he known for?

3. How does Michelangelo's life help you understand Europe during the Renaissance?

4. Who is an artist you admire? Why? Describe how his or her artwork shows religious or secular themes.

The Great Works of
Raphael

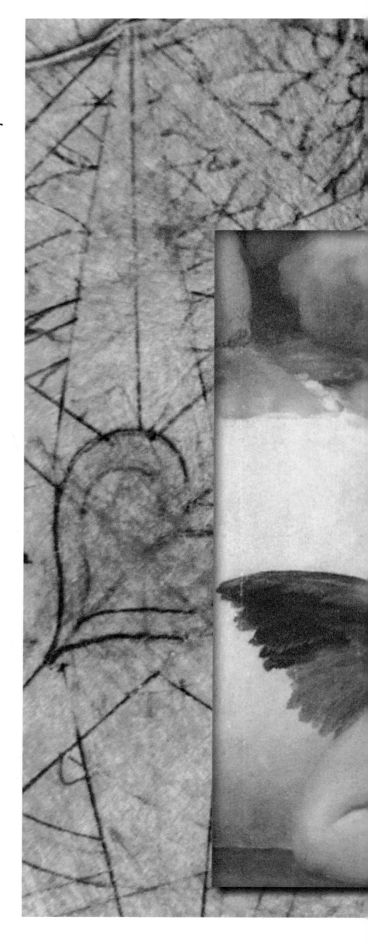

Raphael is considered one of the greatest Renaissance artists. However, he may be best known as the person who painted the images of adorable little angels that today are used to decorate t-shirts, coffee mugs, and calendars. The range of his work is much broader than that. During his short life, Raphael was an artist who painted pictures with strong religious themes as well as ones that reflected secular interests.

■ c. 1495 — Raphael arrives at Perugia to study with Pietro Perugino

A.D. 1490   A.D. 1550

c. 1508 — Pope Julius II invites Raphael to paint the
■ interior ceilings and walls of four rooms in the Sistine Chapel

Raphael created much more than those cute little cupids. In fact, the cupids are only a small part of a larger painting called "Sistine Madonna" (above).

45

Fast Facts

GIVEN NAME: Raphaello Sanzio
BORN: April 1483; Urbino, Italy
DIED: April 1520; Rome, Italy
LIVED: Urbino; Perugia; Florence; Rome
FAMILY: Father, Giovanni Santi; mother, Magia di Battista Ciarla
FAMOUS WORKS: "Sposalizio" (Marriage of the Virgin),
"Disputa" (Disputation Concerning the Holy Sacrament),
"Sistine Madonna"

Urbino— Birthplace of Artists

Some people believe this is what Raphael might have looked like as a young man. It is actually one of Raphael's portraits of a patron, Bindo Altoviti (c. 1515).

The town of Urbino is located in northeastern Italy. For hundreds of years, Urbino and the surrounding area had been known for the great artists who had been born there. However, it was not until 1483 when Raphael—the man who would become the town's greatest and most famous artist—was born. Raphael received his first lessons in painting from his father, Giovanni. In his biography of Raphael, Giorgio Vasari refers to Giovanni as a "painter of no great stature, but an intelligent and kind man." Giovanni quickly realized that he could not give his son all of the art instruction he would need. Fortunately, Giovanni knew one of the best artists in the nearby town of Perugia and made arrangements for Raphael to study with him. Raphael's new teacher would be Pietro Perugino.

Raphael's Apprenticeship in Perugia

The exact date of Raphael's arrival at Perugia is not known. Most historians place the date about 1495. Once Raphael arrived, however, Perugino immediately recognized his talent. During the four years that Raphael studied in Perugia, he learned to imitate Perugino's style. In fact, he became so good at copying Perugino's style that art historians have a difficult time determining whether Raphael created some paintings of this time or whether Perugino painted the works.

Florence Influences Raphael's Style

After several years of working with Perugino, Raphael became aware of two artists living and working in Florence—Leonardo da Vinci and Michelangelo. Raphael heard about two preliminary drawings that these men had done and he was determined to see the drawings for himself. Once Raphael arrived in Florence, he became friends with many of the local artists. During the years 1505-1507, Leonardo da Vinci greatly influenced Raphael's work. Over time, Raphael's style of painting changed. It is clear that he learned a great deal from the Florentine artists and began to use many of their techniques. However, not all artists were happy that Raphael adopted their techniques. Long after Raphael's death, Michelangelo wrote in a letter, "everything he knew about art he got from me."

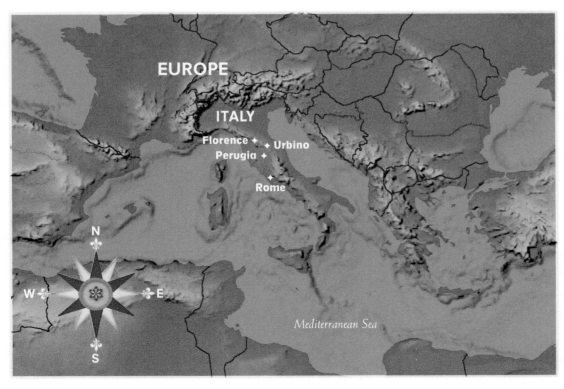

Raphael traveled to different places in Italy learning different artistic styles and techniques.

This illustration shows
Raphael painting the
"Portrait of Maddalena Doni"
(c. 1506).

48

On to Rome

In the fall of 1508, Pope Julius II invited a number of artists to come to Rome. He wanted them to decorate the new Sistine Chapel and his living quarters. Raphael was asked to paint the interior ceilings and walls of four rooms. His work inside the Vatican apartments represents some of the finest examples of Renaissance art. Like many of the artists of the time, Raphael used the faces of people he knew as figures in the backgrounds of his paintings. In 1513, Pope Julius II died. However, the next pope, Leo X, asked Raphael to continue his work. Specifically, the pope wanted Raphael to create paintings that depicted some of the miraculous events in the history of Christianity.

While he was living in Rome and working for the pope, Raphael also was asked by private citizens to paint portraits and other decorative interiors. One of his paintings during this time, the *Portrait of Baldassare Castiglione*, is considered one of the finest works of its type. Castiglione was a very famous author from Raphael's hometown of Urbino. He wrote what some historians think was the most widely read book during the Renaissance—*The Courtier*—a guide for men who wanted to be gentlemen in society. In 1514, Bramante, the man serving as architect for St. Peter's Basilica, died. The pope then asked Raphael if he would take over the work. Raphael agreed. In 1515, the pope asked Raphael to take on more responsibilities. He wanted Raphael to oversee a project that would preserve all of the **antiquities** in Rome. All of the pope's various artistic projects were now under Raphael's supervision.

Raphael's Unfinished Work

The last **masterpiece** credited to Raphael is the "Transfiguration," commissioned in 1517. It shows the moment when Christians believe Jesus changed in appearance and became divine. According to the Bible, Jesus took two of his followers to a mountaintop and there, "his face did shine as the sun and his garments became white as snow." This very large **altarpiece** now hangs in the Vatican Museums. The "Transfiguration" was unfinished when Raphael died in 1520 at the age of 37. His assistant completed it for his master.

Throughout his life, Raphael had been influenced by many of the greatest artists of his time. In each case, he combined his own immense talent with ideas and techniques he had learned from others. The result was the creation of many of the greatest paintings of the Renaissance.

altarpiece: a painting, carving, or other artwork that is placed above or behind an altar

antiquity: item from ancient times, especially the times preceding the Middle Ages

masterpiece: an outstanding work of art or craft

Look to the Source

In 1550, Giorgio Vasari wrote biographies of many important Renaissance artists. Here are a few excerpts from his writing about Raphael.

"Among his many extraordinary gifts, there is one of such value and importance that I can never sufficiently admire it and I always think of it with astonishment. This was his heavenly power of bringing all who came near him into harmony, inconceivably surprising in the nature of an artist, and true only in his presence. This was because all were surpassed by him in friendly courtesy, all confessed the influence of his sweet and gracious nature. Even the very animals followed his steps and always loved him."

"While we may term other works paintings, those of Raphael are living things, the flesh palpitates, the breath comes and goes, every organ lives, life pulsates everywhere."

It is said about Raphael: "When this noble artisan died, painting too might have died, for when he closed his eyes, painting closed his eyes, painting was left almost blind."

Quick Quiz

1. How did Raphael learn the skills to become an artist?

2. Who influenced Raphael's artistic style?

3. As other artists during the Renaissance, Raphael created artwork with both religious and secular themes. Why do you think he did this?

4. What do you think other artists Raphael met thought of him? How is he remembered today?

Like many of the artists of the time, Raphael used the faces of people he knew as figures in the backgrounds of his paintings. This is a re-creation of one of Raphael's paintings that shows Pope Leo X. When Raphael died, it is said that the pope loved him so much that he "wept bitterly at his death."

Sofonisba Anguissola
Artist and Role Model

During the Renaissance, girls did not have many choices about what they would do when they grew up. Most girls of noble birth were expected to marry. And most of these girls spent their time waiting for marriage doing things such as sewing. Only a few exceptional girls became well educated or went on to become important artists. Sofonisba Anguissola is one such woman. She did not follow the traditional role of women in Renaissance society. She became well known as an excellent portrait painter.

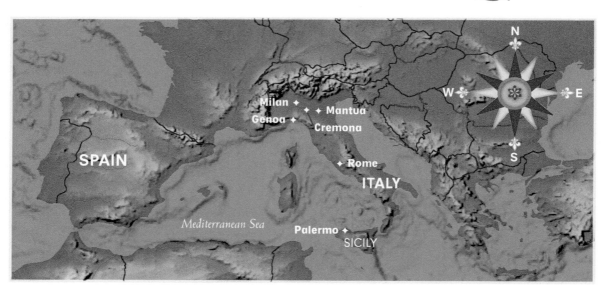

c. 1554 — Sofonisba goes to Rome and meets Michelangelo

c. 1560 — Philip II of Spain asks Sofonisba to paint pictures of the Spanish royal family

A.D. 1500   A.D. 1600

Sofonisba Anguissola is best known for the portraits she painted. Almost all the people in her paintings are happy and smiling. Other painters of the time tended to show people as being very serious.

53

GIVEN NAME: Sofonisba Anguissola
BORN: c. 1532 in Cremona, Italy
DIED: 1625 in Palermo, Sicily
LIVED: Italy and Spain
FAMILY: Father, Amilcare Anguissola; mother, Bianca Ponzone; five sisters; one brother; married twice; no children
FAMOUS WORKS: "Portrait of the Artist's Sister Minerva," "Self Portrait," "Bernardino Campi Painting Sofonisba Anguissola," "The Chess Game"

Fast Facts

Sofonisba Anguissola painted more self-portraits than anyone else of her time.

The Daughter of an Artist

Sofonisba was born around 1532 in Cremona, a city in northern Italy about 40 miles southwest of Milan. Her parents, Bianca Ponzone and Amilcare Anguissola, were part of the noble class. Sofonisba was the first of their six daughters. Their seventh child was a son. Sofonisba's father was a humanist who wanted his children to have a fine education. They studied many different subjects, including art and music. Like many young girls of the time, Sofonisba and her sisters learned how to paint. Over time, she and her sisters became excellent painters and musicians.

When she was about 14 years old, Sofonisba's father arranged for her and one of his other daughters to study painting under the direction of Bernardino Campi. Campi was a well-respected artist and he and his wife welcomed the girls to their family's home. The girls remained there for three years, learning how to mix pigments and prepare canvases for painting, and endlessly sketching plants, animals, and people.

When her teacher left for Milan in 1546, Sofonisba began to study with Bernardino Gatti, another artist in Cremona. She became quite an accomplished painter and began to teach her younger sisters.

An Innovative Painter

As a young woman, Sofonisba painted pictures of herself and her sisters. In fact, she painted more self-portraits than any other artist at the time. Thirteen of these self-portraits still exist. Even at an early age, she was an **innovative** painter. One of her most famous paintings shows three of her sisters playing chess. What is very different about this picture is that the sisters are smiling. Most other artists of the time painted pictures of people with very serious looks on their faces.

Around 1554, Sofonisba went to Rome. While she was there, she met Michelangelo. She was in her early twenties and he would have been almost 80 years old. He gave her several of his sketches to copy and she sent him samples of her work. He suggested she sketch a picture of a boy who was crying. Her sketch was excellent and it was much discussed and copied for years. Giorgio Vasari, who wrote a brief biography of Sofonisba, described the sketch in this way: "One could not see a more graceful or realistic drawing than this one." In an informal way, Michelangelo guided her study of art and her development as an artist. Several years after this visit, Sofonisba's father, Amilcare Anguissola, wrote a letter to Michelangelo thanking him for helping his daughter. He wrote that Michelangelo was "such a great and talented gentleman…[and] was kind enough to examine, judge, and praise the paintings done by my daughter, Sofonisba."

After Sofonisba returned to Cremona, she spent most of her time painting. Sometimes she traveled to other Italian cities such as Mantua or Milan to paint portraits of noble families. Since she was unmarried, she always traveled with one or more of her sisters, servants, and a **chaperone**.

Spain Welcomes Sofonisba

Over time, Sofonisba Anguissola's importance as an artist grew. She had become a well-respected portrait painter. It was wonderful, but not surprising, when Philip II, king of Spain, invited her to come to his court. He wanted her to paint pictures of the Spanish royal family. He also thought she might be a good companion and teacher for his 15-year-old bride, Isabel. For the next 10-20 years (historians are not exactly sure), Sofonisba lived and worked in Spain. She became a friend and teacher of the young queen and also was an official court painter. The king and queen paid her well for her services. She received silks, embroidered velvets, gold and silver threads, and other valuables that were used as **currency**.

chaperone: a person, usually an older or married woman, who supervises or accompanies a young unmarried woman in public

currency: any form of money used as a medium of exchange

innovative: creative

Finding True Love

When she was about 38 years old, King Philip arranged for Sofonisba to marry Don Fabrizio de Moncada, an Italian noble from Sicily. The couple traveled to Italy after their marriage, but then returned to Spain for several years. Around 1578, they moved to Sicily for good, but Sofonisba's husband died of the **plague** there in 1579. Now a widow, Sofonisba decided to return to her family home in Cremona. She had to travel by ship from the island of Sicily to the Italian mainland. While onboard the ship, she met the captain, Orazio Lomellino. They developed a friendship and then married in 1580. Sofonisba moved with her husband to Genoa, his family home. He was very supportive of Sofonisba's work as an artist. She had her own art studio and welcomed many artists to visit, discuss art, and share their learning.

international recognition: favorable attention or notice spread beyond a single country

plague: a highly infectious, usually deadly, disease

Sofonisba did not follow the traditional role of women in Renaissance society. She became a role model for other women during that time.

A Role Model

Sofonisba Anguissola came to be regarded as a role model for other women artists. She is most famous for her portrait paintings, but in her later years she also painted many pictures that had religious themes. During her life, Sofonisba probably painted more than 50 pictures. No one knows for sure how many paintings she actually created. Art historians believe that only a small portion of her work still exists. Sofonisba Anguissola enjoyed **international recognition** for most of her life and lived to a very old age. She died in 1625 and was buried in Palermo, Sicily.

Look to the Source

In 1632, seven years after her death, Sofonisba's second husband had an inscription carved on her tomb. His message read, "To Sofonisba, my wife ... who is recorded among the illustrious women of the world, outstanding in portraying the images of man ... Orazio Lomellino, in sorrow for the loss of his great love, dedicated this little tribute to such a great woman."

Giorgio Vasari praised Sofonisba Anguissola in his book, *The Lives of the Artists*, written in the mid-1500s. He commented on the favor the king of Spain showed Sofonisba: "[He] supports her in the queen's company with a huge provision, to the amazement of all his court which admires as a wondrous thing Sophonisba's excellence."

Note: Vasari spelled her name "Sophonisba."

Quick Quiz

1. What advantages and disadvantages did Sofonisba face as an artist during the Renaissance? How did she overcome her disadvantages?
2. Who supported and encouraged Sofonisba's artistic pursuits?
3. What made Sofonisba an exceptional girl?
4. Why is Sofonisba considered an exceptional artist?

NORTH AMERICA

ATLANTIC OCEAN

The Renaissance Spreads

By 1475, the ideas of the Italian Renaissance had spread to northern Europe by word of mouth and also through books and other written materials. By 1500, European printers were publishing books on many subjects in different languages. More people learned to read. They learned about new ideas and about new ways of understanding the world.

BELGIUM

NETHERLANDS

GERMANY

FRANCE

EUROPE

ASIA

ITALY

SPAIN

Mediterranean Sea

AFRICA

N

W — E

S

Adapting Renaissance Ideas in New Settings

By the mid-1500s, the ideas of the Renaissance had become popular throughout Europe. People in northern Europe **adapted** these ideas according to their own traditions. They brought together ancient ideas of human reason with religious themes. The ideas of the Italian Renaissance influenced artists in northern Europe who created artwork in the tradition of the Italian Renaissance. Their work is realistic, full of human passion, and very creative. Two examples of artists from northern Europe who were greatly influenced by ideas of the Italian Renaissance are Jan van Eyck, a **Flemish** painter, and Albrecht Dürer, a German painter and printmaker. Artemisia Gentileschi was an Italian artist who worked during the time after the Renaissance. Her work is an example of how Renaissance ideas and techniques continued to influence artists for years to come.

adapt: to become accustomed to

Flemish: from Flanders, an area that is now part of the countries France and Belgium

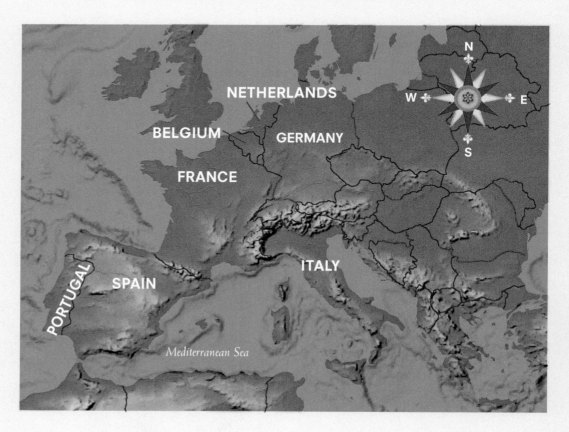

The ideas of the Italian Renaissance quickly spread throughout Europe.

People in northern Europe adapted Renaissance ideas according to their own traditions. They were interested in bringing together ancient ideas of human reason with religious themes.

Jan van Eyck— Master of Oil Paintings

Jan van Eyck was born around 1390 and worked in the Netherlands, northern France, and Belgium. From 1422-1424, he was an important court painter for Count John of Bavaria. The following year, he accepted an invitation to be the court painter for Duke Philip the Good of Burgundy. As a member of the duke's court, Jan van Eyck also sometimes served as a diplomat. For example, he went on one secret mission to Spain and Portugal with the goal of arranging a marriage for the duke with Isabella of Portugal. Jan van Eyck often has been given credit for the invention of painting in oils. This is not true, but he certainly was an important figure in improving the technique of oil painting. He and his brother Hubert, also an artist, discovered that by mixing their pigments in oil instead of an egg medium, they ended up with colors that were bright, clean, and intense. Jan van Eyck's oil paintings are very accurate and detailed. Everything looks real! Even the images of jewels and metals that appear in his paintings seem to glow. He achieved this effect by painting a **glaze** over them. Art historians often comment on the way he painted backgrounds in pictures to create a feeling of space. He painted religious and secular pictures. Jan van Eyck died in 1441 and is remembered as one of the greatest painters of all time.

glaze: a thin, shiny, smooth coat

Albrecht Dürer was a Renaissance artist outside of Italy. This picture of the German artist was created in the mid-1800s.

Apocalypse: the last book of the New Testament, also known as Revelations; refers to a revelation (something that is revealed or shown) of what is to come in the future

Albrecht Dürer—The Greatest Printmaker of His Time

Albrecht Dürer was born in 1471 in Nuremberg, Germany. His father was a goldsmith and Dürer trained to become a metalworker himself. As a young man he visited Venice and came home a changed man. Leonardo da Vinci's works greatly influenced him. Dürer was a painter, writer, and most importantly the greatest printmaker of his time. His work is known for its attention to detail. Like other Renaissance artists, Dürer's work reflected both religious and secular themes. One of his most important works is a woodcut print called "Four Horsemen of the **Apocalypse**," which he created in 1497-1498. This relates to a description of the coming of a Day of Judgment in the New Testament of the Bible. Four horsemen ride out. One symbolizes conquering power, the second represents war, the third is famine, and the fourth is death. The original work hangs in the Metropolitan Museum of Art in New York. Dürer's later work showed his growing enthusiasm for Martin Luther and his ideas about religion. Dürer died in 1528, leaving as his legacy many beautiful works of art that continue to be admired today.

"I find myself with a female daughter and three other sons, and this daughter, as it pleased God, having been trained in the profession of painting, in three years had become so skilled that I dare say she has no equal today, for she has made works that demonstrates a level of understanding that perhaps the leading masters of the profession have not attained."

—*Orazio Gentileschi said this to a patron assuring her that his daughter, Artemisia, was a very talented painter.*

Artemisia Gentileschi— An Exceptional Painter

Artemisia Gentileschi created praised paintings during the period of time that came after the Renaissance. Like Sofonisba Anguissola, Artemisia was an exceptional painter. Her work was greatly influenced by the Italian Renaissance. Until recently, however, Artemisia did not receive the kind of popular or critical interest that was directed toward Renaissance artists. More attention, it seems, was focused on a scandal in her personal life—when Gentileschi was a young artist, she was assaulted by her tutor during one of her art lessons. In the last few decades, art historians have begun to take more careful notice of Artemisia's artistry and have come to appreciate the genius of her work.

Much of what we know about where Artemisia lived is linked to her painting. In Genoa, there are two signed works by her that are dated between 1621-1622. Because Genoa was such a wealthy city, there were many people who could afford to buy her paintings. However, by the end of 1622, she had returned to Rome. During the time Artemisia lived in Rome, Urban VIII was pope. This was a creative and exciting period for artists living in Rome. One of the most well-known artists, Bernini, was working on the interior of St. Peter's Basilica. In 1630, Artemisia produced one of her most famous works, "Self Portrait as the Allegory of Painting." This picture was purchased by King Charles I of England.

pioneer: to open up new areas of thought, research, and development

Artemisia had various patrons for her work. However, for the last 10 years of her life, she did most of her work for a single patron, Don Antonio Ruffo. She completed several fine paintings, which continued to have strong women as their central figure. She died in 1653. Although some writers of her time mentioned her in their works, for the most part she was ignored. Perhaps this is because she did not paint many of the public works that are used to recognize more famous painters of her time. In the early 1900s, an essay was written about Artemisia. Since then, she has become more and more well known.

Continuing Influences of the Italian Renaissance

Other artists including Peter Paul Rubens and Rembrandt from the Netherlands, the Spaniard El Greco from Crete, and many, many others also were influenced by Renaissance art and ideas. Indeed, artists up to this very day continue to admire and be inspired by the work of Renaissance artists. They also rely on many of the principles such as perspective that Renaissance artists **pioneered**. And like Renaissance artists, people today continue to experiment with new art forms and media and they express their ideas in both religious and secular creations.

Quick Quiz

1. Name some of the Renaissance ideas that influenced artists outside of Italy and artists who came after the Italian Renaissance.

2. Do you think Renaissance ideas exist in our society today? Do you agree with Renaissance ideas? Why or why not?

Rembrandt and other artists who came after the Renaissance were greatly influenced by the art created during that period. Rembrandt painted this self-portrait in 1640.

READER'S THEATER PRESENTS:

What Will Become of this Boy?

ROLES

- ★ **NARRATOR 1**
- ★ **NARRATOR 2**
- ★ **ALL**
- ★ **TOWNSMEN**
- ★ **TOWNSWOMEN**
- ★ **UNCLE FRANCESCO**
- ★ **LEONARDO**

NARRATOR 1: On April 15, 1452, a boy named Leonardo was born. His father was a leading citizen of the community. He was responsible for preparing legal documents. This was an important job.

NARRATOR 2: But Leonardo's mother was only a peasant girl. And she was not married to Leonardo's father.

ALL: What difference did that make?

NARRATOR 2: Well, that meant Leonardo could not go to the university. He could not become a doctor or lawyer or a banker.

NARRATOR 1: This might have been a terrible problem for other boys. However, young Leonardo was quite different.

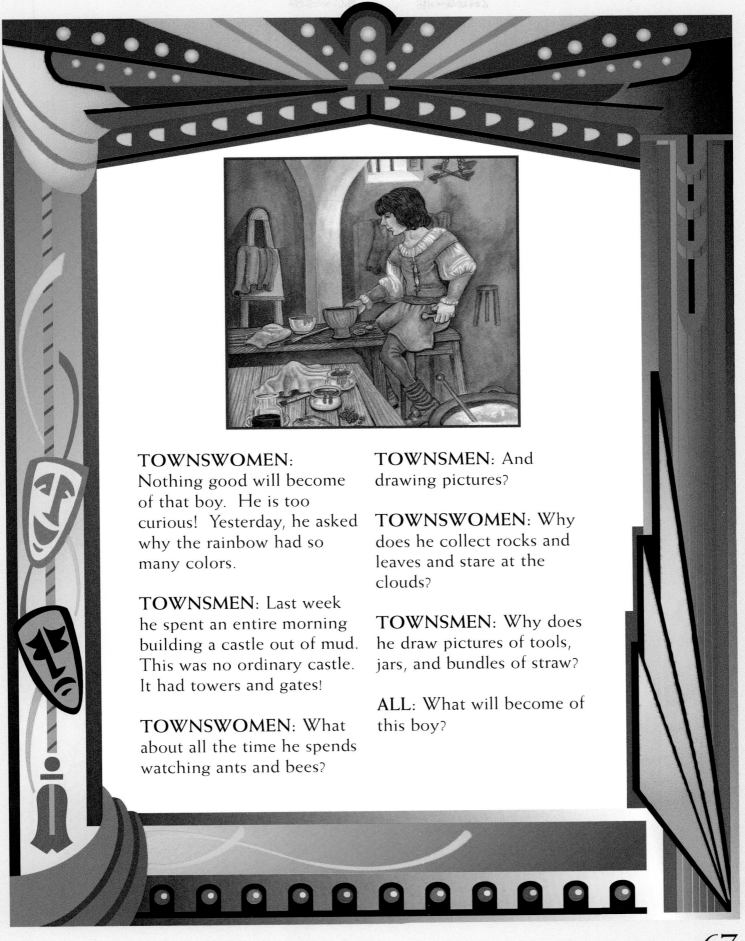

TOWNSWOMEN:
Nothing good will become of that boy. He is too curious! Yesterday, he asked why the rainbow had so many colors.

TOWNSMEN: Last week he spent an entire morning building a castle out of mud. This was no ordinary castle. It had towers and gates!

TOWNSWOMEN: What about all the time he spends watching ants and bees?

TOWNSMEN: And drawing pictures?

TOWNSWOMEN: Why does he collect rocks and leaves and stare at the clouds?

TOWNSMEN: Why does he draw pictures of tools, jars, and bundles of straw?

ALL: What will become of this boy?

UNCLE FRANCESCO:
Stop it! I am proud of
Leonardo. He is a bright
and curious boy. Some day
you will see how wrong
you are about him!

LEONARDO: Thank you,
Uncle Francesco, for believing
in me. Come quick. I want to
show you the flying machine I
made. I am going to fly like a
bird!

ALL: Oh no. A flying
machine?

NARRATOR 1: Some
people thought Leonardo
would never become
successful.

NARRATOR 2: They
thought he would never
choose one thing and
become really good at it.

ALL: Were they right?

NARRATOR 1: Yes and no.

NARRATOR 2: Leonardo did not choose to do one thing. He decided to do many things—engineering, architecture, painting, and inventing. He even designed costumes!

NARRATOR 1: And he became very good at all these things. He wrote pages and pages of notes about his ideas. And he drew lots of pictures of his ideas.

ALL: Can we read his notes?

NARRATOR 2: You can if you have a mirror and know Italian.

ALL: Why do we need a mirror?

NARRATOR 1: Because Leonardo wrote his notes backwards.

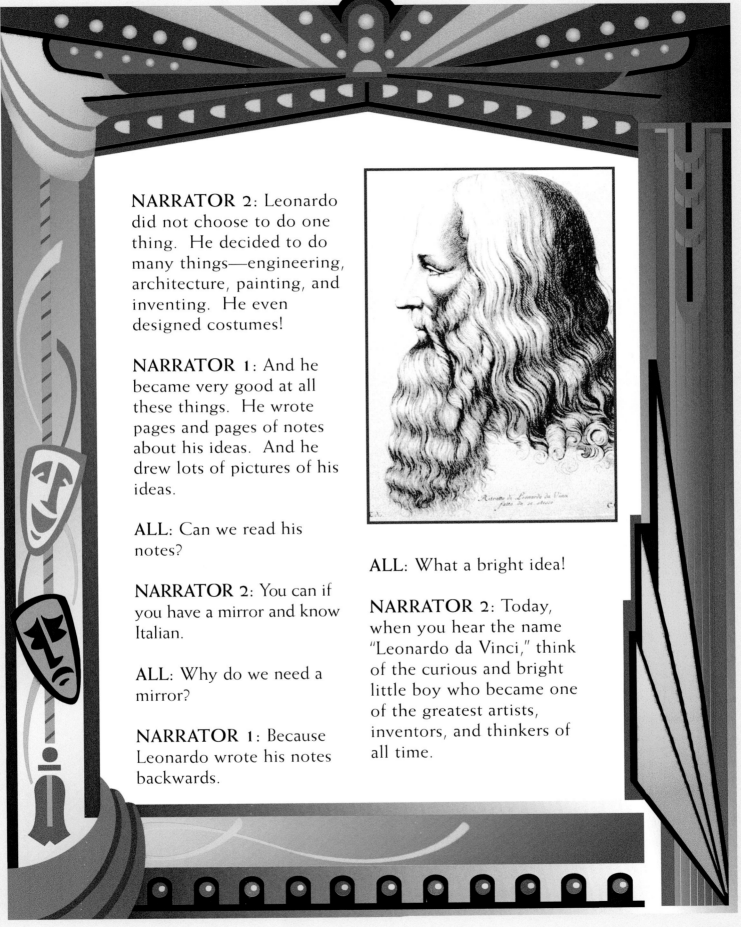

Retratto di Leonardo da Vinci
fatto da se stesso

ALL: What a bright idea!

NARRATOR 2: Today, when you hear the name "Leonardo da Vinci," think of the curious and bright little boy who became one of the greatest artists, inventors, and thinkers of all time.

69

Activities

After you have read one or more of the chapters in this book, take part in one of these activities and make history come alive! You can do these on your own or with friends and family members.

PORTRAITS – Choose one of the people you read about in this book. Draw an outline of the person's profile. Inside the profile, write biographical information about the person, including when he or she lived and why he or she is remembered.

ALIKE OR DIFFERENT – Choose one of the people you read about in this book. Then think about how that person's life and the time in which that person lived is alike or different from your life today. Write this information on a Venn diagram. Analyze how the two eras are alike and different, as well as how your life is alike and different from the historical figure you chose.

A LETTER TO A FRIEND – The people who lived in the past were real people. They enjoyed advantages, but also encountered hardships and obstacles. Choose one of the people you read about in this book. Then write a letter to a friend that starts, "I met an amazing artist today. Let me tell you about …" In your letter, be sure to tell what you admired about the artist, how the person's artwork reflected secular and/or religious themes, advantages the person enjoyed, obstacles the person overcame, and words you would use to describe the person's character.

POETIC LICENSE – Choose one of the people you read about in this book. Write a poem about the artist on a piece of paper that is cut in the shape of a picture frame or some other symbol of an artist. Follow the pattern below:

Line 1: The person's name
Line 2: One word to describe the person
Line 3: Two words to describe the person
Line 4: Three words to describe the person
Line 5: The person's name

POSTER ART – Choose one of the people you read about in this book. Then create a "Moment in Time" poster showing one day in the person's life.

A PERSON TO REMEMBER – Choose one of the people you read about in this book. Then prepare a one-page report entitled, "A Person to Remember." Be sure to include the following information in your report:

Personal Information (year born, family, education, social class)

Description (how the person looked)

Character Traits (qualities the person possessed)

Achievements (what the person accomplished)

Descriptive Words (words you would use to describe the person)

Your Opinion (your opinion of the person)

CROSSWORD PUZZLER – Choose one or more of the people you read about in this book and create a crossword puzzle using words associated with the person or people. Here's an example!

ACROSS

1. A famous "smiling" painting
2. Leonardo's "The _____ Supper"
3. At the very end of paint brushes are the _____
4. The period during which Raphael lived and worked is called the _____
5. Some people thought Michelangelo was a _____
6. The king of Spain asked this artist to be court painter

DOWN

1. A worker who cuts stone is called a _____
7. Some artists use marble; others use _____
8. A famous Botticelli painting is called "Adoration of the _____"
9. Lorenzo di Medici was an important _____ of artists
10. People who create artwork are called _____
11. The period in Europe before the Renaissance is called the Middle _____
12. During the Renaissance, the _____ flourished
13. Michelangelo's famous sculpture; means "pity" in Italian

Answers:

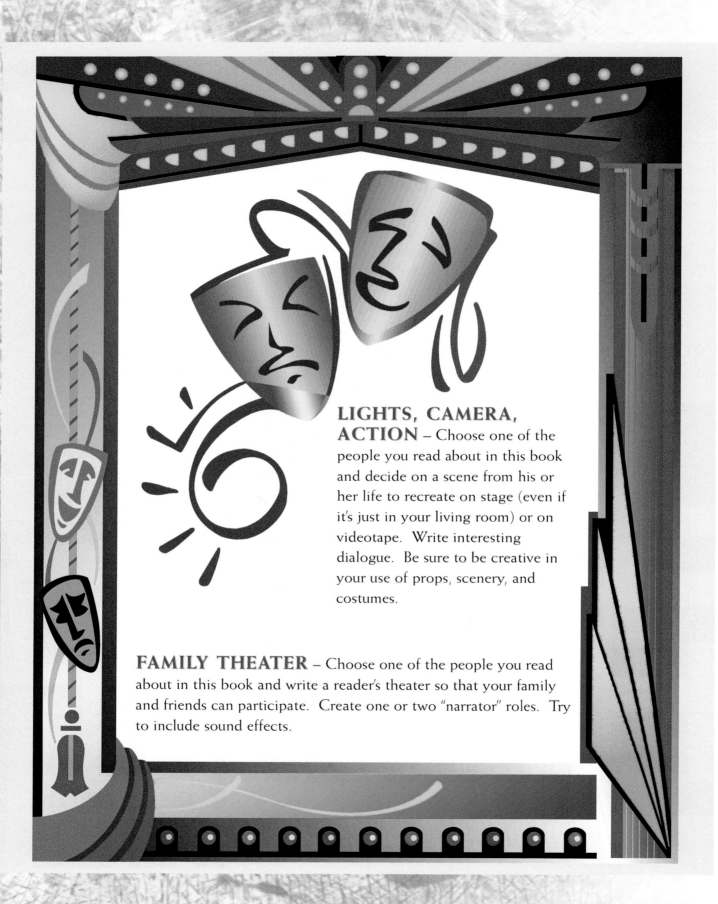

LIGHTS, CAMERA, ACTION – Choose one of the people you read about in this book and decide on a scene from his or her life to recreate on stage (even if it's just in your living room) or on videotape. Write interesting dialogue. Be sure to be creative in your use of props, scenery, and costumes.

FAMILY THEATER – Choose one of the people you read about in this book and write a reader's theater so that your family and friends can participate. Create one or two "narrator" roles. Try to include sound effects.

Test Your Knowledge!

PICK THE RIGHT ANSWER! (1 POINT EACH)

1. Where did the Renaissance begin?
   a. France
   b. Italy
   c. England

2. What general period of time does the Renaissance cover?
   a. 509 B.C. – the fall of Rome (476)
   b. the fall of Rome (476) – 1350
   c. 1350 - 1600

3. On what continent is Italy located?
   a. Africa
   b. Asia
   c. Europe

4. Who is known as the "father of the Renaissance"?
   a. Sandro Botticelli
   b. Francesco Petrarch
   c. Michelangelo

WHO AM I? (1 POINT EACH)

5. I created a famous statue of David (of David and Goliath fame) and also painted pictures from Biblical scenes on the ceiling of the Sistine Chapel.

   Who am I? _____

6. I painted pictures of people with smiles on their faces. I also became a role model for women artists.

   Who am I? _____

MAKE A MATCH! (1 POINT EACH)

7. republic
8. biography
9. chapel
10. diplomat
11. chisel
12. masterpiece
13. plague
14. genius
15. patron

a. a written account of a person's life; a life history
b. a form of government where people choose their leaders
c. a person who represents a government with other governments
d. an outstanding work of art
e. a person who supports, protects, or champions something
f. a person with exceptional intelligence or creativity
g. to cut stone, wood, or metal using a sharp-edged tool
h. a highly infectious, usually deadly, disease
i. a small church

WHAT'S YOUR SCORE?

14-15 points – TOP SCORE!
12-13 points – Good
10-11 points – Fair
Fewer than 9 points? Time to read the book again!

Answers: 1b, 2c, 3c, 4b; 5-Michelangelo, 6-Sofonisba Anguissola; 7b, 8a, 9i, 10c, 11g, 12d, 13h, 14f, 15e

Glossary

altarpiece: (AWL-tur-pees) *n*. A painting, carving, or other artwork that is placed above or behind an altar.

anatomy: (uh-NAT-uh-mee). *n*. The structure of an animal or plant or of any of its parts.

antiquity: (an-TIK-wuh-tee) *n*. Item from ancient times, especially the times preceding the Middle Ages.

Apocalypse: (uh-PAHK-uh-lips) *n*. The last book of the New Testament, also known as Revelations; refers to a revelation (something that is revealed or shown) of what is to come in the future.

apprentice: (uh-PREN-tis) *n*. A person who goes to work for another person; in return for this work, the apprentice learns a trade, art, or business.

biography: (biy-OG-ruh-fee) *n*. A written account of a person's life; a life history.

bonfire of the vanities: (BON-fiyr uv thee VAN-uh-tees) *n*. A large outdoor fire in which items that are not considered "useful" or worthwhile are burned.

chapel: (CHAP-ul) *n*. A small church.

PARTS OF SPEECH KEY

n. — **noun; a noun is a word that names a person, place, thing, or quality**
Examples: monk, Vatican, altarpiece, humanism, recognition

adj. — **adjective; an adjective is a word that describes, limits, qualifies, or specifies a person, place, thing, quality, or act**
Examples: secular, innovative, international, literary, modest

v. — **verb; a verb is a word that expresses action, occurrence, or existence**
Examples: commission, conduct, dissect, struggle

chaperone: (SHAP-uh-rohn) *n*. A person, usually an older or married woman, who supervises or accompanies a young unmarried woman in public.

chisel: (CHIZ-ul) *v*. To cut and shape stone, wood, or metal using a metal tool with a sharp edge.

cloak: (klohk) *n*. A loose outer garment without sleeves; like a cape.

commission: (kuh-MISH-un) *v*. To place an order for.

conduct: (kun-DUKT) *v*. To direct or control.

currency: (KUR-un-see) *n*. Any form of money used as a medium of exchange.

diplomat: (DIP-luh-mat) *n*. A person who represents a government in relations with other governments.

dissect: (di-SEKT) *v*. To cut apart, especially for study.

Fra: (fraw) *n*. Brother; a title given to an Italian friar or monk; abbreviation of the Italian word *frate*.

Flemish: (FLEM-ish) *adj*. From Flanders, an area that is now part of the countries France and Belgium.

fresco: (FRES-koh) *n*. An artwork created by painting on damp plaster with watercolor paints.

guild: (gild) *n*. An organization of people of the same trade or interests; people form guilds for protection, to maintain standards, or for other purposes.

humanism: (HYOO-muh-niz-um) *n*. A way of thinking that is concerned with human achievement and a belief in the importance of individual power, dignity, and the ability to improve through education.

innovative: (in-uh-VAY-tiv) *adj*. Creative.

international recognition: (in-tur-NASH-uh-nul rek-uhg-NISH-un) *adj./n*. Favorable attention or notice spread beyond a single country.

literary: (LIT-uh-rer-ee) *adj*. Relating to literature (written works).

marble: (MAHR-bul) *n.* A kind of rock used for sculpture and architectural decoration.

mason: (MAY-sun) *n.* A person who builds or works with stone or brick.

masterpiece: (MAS-tuhr-pees) *n.* An outstanding work of art or craft.

modest: (MOD-ist) *adj.* Have a shy or reserved manner; quiet and humble.

monk: (munk) *n.* A man who pursues a life of religious service.

patron: (PAY-trun) *n.* A person who supports, protects, or champions something.

perspective: (pur-SPEK-tiv) *n.* A technique (based on mathematical principles) of making some objects look closer and others appear farther away.

pigment: (PIG-munt) *n.* Any substance used as coloring; pigments are usually mixed with water, oil, or another base to produce paint.

pioneer: (piy-uh-NEER) *v.* To open up new areas of thought, research, and development.

plague: (playg) *n.* A highly infectious, usually deadly, disease.

Renaissance: (REN-I-sahns) *n.* A French word meaning "rebirth"; refers to a revival of ancient Greek and Roman art, literature, and learning that began in Italy in the 1350s and spread throughout Europe; the term *Renaissance* was first used by a French historian, Jules Michelet (c. 1793-1874), to refer to the "discovery of the world and of man" in the 1500s.

republic: (ri-PUB-lik) *n.* A form of government where people choose their leaders.

secular: (SEK-yuh-lur) *adj.* Not specifically related to religion or to a religious body.

slingshot: (SLING-shawt) *n.* A Y-shaped stick with a strap attached to fling small stones.

St. Peter's Basilica: (saynt PEE-turz buh-SIL-i-kuh) *n.* A Christian church named after Peter, one of Jesus's 12 followers; after his death, Peter was named a saint (abbreviation is St.) for having lived a holy life.

struggle: (STRUG-ul) *v.* To make a strong effort to solve a problem.

tyrant: (TIY-runt) *n.* A ruler who uses power in a harsh, cruel way.

Vatican: (VAT-i-kun) *n.* The official residence (or home) of the pope; the Vatican is located in Vatican City, an independent state located within the city of Rome.

VOWEL PRONUNCIATION KEY

SYMBOL	KEY WORDS
a	ant, man
ay	cake, May
ah	clock, arm
aw	salt, ball
ayr	hair, bear
e	neck, bed
ee	ear, key
i	chick, skin
iy	five, tiger
oh	coat, soda
oi	boy, coin
ohr	board, door
oo	blue, boot
ow	cow, owl
u	foot, wolf, bird, and the schwa sound used in final syllables followed by 'l', 'r', 's', 'm', 't', or 'n'
uh	bug, uncle, and other schwa sounds

The vowel pronunciation key is derived from the following three sources: *American Heritage Dictionary of the English Language*, 1981; *Oxford American Dictionary: Heald Colleges Edition*, 1982; *Webster's New World College Dictionary, Third Edition*, 1990.

Index

Skills Index/Credits

SKILLS INDEX

CONTENT LINKS

Anthropology (culture) 8-9, 13-15, 17, 20-21, 25-26, 28-29, 33, 37, 44, 47, 52, 54

Economics 13-15, 20, 24, 34, 39, 55

Geography 4-5, 11, 20, 22, 29, 34-39, 47, 52, 58-59, 60

Government 13, 21, 55

History 4-65

Language Arts/Literature 10, 14, 15, 22, 23-25, 32, 36, 38, 40, 43, 49-50, 55, 57

Religion/Philosophy 13-14, 16, 21-22, 30, 40-41, 43, 49, 60-61, 21

Science 13-14, 17, 29, 30-31, 61

Visual/Performing Arts, including art history, architecture, and music 9-70, 72

CHRONOLOGICAL AND SPATIAL THINKING

Understand key events and people of the historical era they are studying both in a chronological sequence and within a spatial context. 6-65

Identify how the present is connected to the past, identifying both similarities and differences between the two, and how some things change over time and some things stay the same. 4-5, 17, 23, 43, 50, 57, 70

LANGUAGE DEVELOPMENT

Develop vocabulary 10-11, 13, 15, 17, 20-24, 28-29, 31-33, 38, 40, 49, 55-56, 61,71, 73, 74-75; context clues/develop vocabulary in context 11, 14, 16, 18, 20, 30, 47, 49, 50, 57, 70-71

Comprehend figurative language/idioms 8, 10-11, 13, 17-18, 22, 24, 32, 40-41, 47, 49, 50-51, 55, 57, 60-63

Comprehend reading material 17, 24, 33, 41, 48, 55, 72, 73

Think critically 17, 24, 35, 43, 50, 57, 70-71

RESEARCH, EVIDENCE, AND POINT OF VIEW

Read primary sources. 10, 22, 25, 32, 34, 40-41, 43, 46-47, 48-49, 50-51, 55, 57

Pose questions about events encountered in historical documents, eyewitness accounts, oral histories, letters, diaries, artifacts, photographs, maps, artwork, and architecture. 16, 23, 25, 27, 30, 34, 40, 43, 50, 70

Conduct Research. 72-74

Interpret and analyze historical artifacts and accounts; examine conclusions, cause/effect relationships and historical processes. 8-10, 12, 14-16, 21, 23, 25, 30-33, 36-43, 50, 55-57, 59, 61, 63

Develop historical empathy. 24, 35, 43, 50, 57

ACADEMIC STUDY SKILLS

Acquire information by reading various forms of literature and primary and secondary source materials. 4, 8-74

Read and interpret maps, charts, and pictures. 4-9, 11-12, 14-16, 18-23, 25, 27-35, 37, 39-42, 44-48, 51-54, 58-60, 62-63, 65

Understand the specialized academic language used in academic discourse, particularly in the social sciences. 8, 10-11, 13, 15, 17, 22, 25, 32, 49, 55-56

Organize and express ideas clearly in writing and in speaking. 70-74

PICTURE CREDITS

(t=top, b=bottom, c=center, r=right, l=left)

Library of Congress (color by Fred Sherman) cover (l, c), 1, 3 (Michelangelo, Rembrandt), 5 (tr, br), 12, 16, 21, 33 (l), 40 (l), 41, 42, 45, 46, 54, 65

Dover Publications 56

Allison Mangrum 3 (tl), 8-9, 15, 40 (r)

Tamineh Nassiri 35 (l)

Northwind Picture Archives (color by Fred Sherman and Ronaldo Benaraw) 14, 33 (r), 62

pdimages.com 5 (tl), 30, 31, 32, 35 (r), 23, 68, 69

TEXT CREDITS

10 I Cannot Get Enough Books: From *Letters from Petrarch*, translated by Morris Bishop, Indiana University Press, 1966. 22 Giorgio Vasari, *The Lives of the Artists*, translated by Julia Conaway Bondanella and Peter Bondanella, Oxford University Press, 1998. 25 Giorgio Vasari, *The Lives of the Artists*, abridged and edited by Betty Borroughs. New York: Simon and Schuster, 1946. 32 Giorgio Vasari, *The Lives of the Artists*, translated by Julia Conaway Bondanella and Peter Bondanella, Oxford University Press, 1998; Atchitt, Kenneth J. (ed.), *The Renaissance Reader*, New York: Harper Collins, 1996. 40 Bull, G.A., *Michelangelo's Life, Letters, and Poetry*, Oxford University Press, 1999. 41 Giorgio Vasari, *The Lives of the Artists*, translated by Julia Conaway Bondanella and Peter Bondanella, Oxford University Press, 1998. 43, 47 *The Letters of Michelangelo*, translated, edited, and annotated by E.H. Ramsden, Stanford, CA: Stanford University Press, 1963. 49 *The NIV Study Bible*, Kenneth Barker (general editor), Grand Rapids, MI: Zondervan Publishing House, 1995. 50-51, 55 Giorgio Vasari, *The Lives of the Artists*, translated by Julia Conaway Bondanella and Peter Bondanella, Oxford University Press, 1998. 57 Perlingieri, Ilya Sandra, *Sofonisba Anguissola: The First Great Woman Artist of the Renaissance*, New York: Rizzoli International Publications, 1992. 63 Bissel, R. Ward, *Artemisia Gentileschi and the Authority of Art*, University Park, PA: The Pennsylvania University Press, 1999.

77

Find Out More!

FIND MORE RESOURCES
on our web site
**www.ballard-tighe.com/
readingbookactivities**

SANDRO BOTTICELLI:

Venezia, Mike. *Botticelli*. Chicago: Childrens Press, 1991. This book is part of the "Getting to Know the World's Greatest Artists" series and provides a simple biography of Sandro Botticelli, the man who painted "The Birth of Venus." Lots of great pictures and some funny cartoons. Nonfiction.

LEONARDO DA VINCI:

Herbert, Janis. *Leonardo da Vinci for Kids: His Life and Ideas: 21 Activities*. Chicago: Chicago Review Press, 1998. This book tells the story of Leonardo da Vinci using his own words and pictures. You'll also find 21 activities for you to try. Includes a time line, a listing of web sites to explore, and information about where to find Leonardo da Vinci's original works. A Notable Social Studies Trade Book for Young People. Nonfiction.

Romei, Francesca. *Leonardo Da Vinci: Artist, Inventor, and Scientist of the Renaissance* (Masters of Art series). New York: Peter Bedrick Books, 2000. This book provides a broad overview of Leonardo da Vinci and 15th-century Italy. Each double-page spread deals with a specific topic and includes text and an illustration or reproduction. Nonfiction.

Stanley, Diane. *Leonardo da Vinci*. New York: Morrow, 1996. This is the story of Leonardo da Vinci. Lots of information about Florence during the Renaissance. Bulletin Blue Ribbon Book, American Library Association Notable Books for Children, Orbis Pictus Award for Outstanding Nonfiction for Children, and School Library Journal Best Book. Nonfiction.

MICHELANGELO:

Richmond, Robin. *Introducing Michelangelo*. Boston: Little, Brown, 1992. This is an easy-to-read biography of Michelangelo. Emphasis is on the restoration of his frescoes in the Sistine Chapel. Nonfiction.

Spence, David. *Michelangelo and the Renaissance* (Great Artists series). New York: Barron's, 1997. This is a brief, well-written book about one of the greatest artists of the period. Lots of good reproductions of artwork. Nonfiction.

Venezia, Mike. *Michelangelo*. Chicago: Childrens Press, 1991. This is a very easy-to-read biography of the great Renaissance artist. Lots of pictures and a few funny cartoons. Nonfiction.

RAPHAEL:

Merlo, Claudio. *Three Masters of the Renaissance: Leonardo, Michelangelo, Raphael* (Bravo series). New York: Barron's, 1999. This book looks at three important artists of the Italian Renaissance—Leonardo da Vinci, Michelangelo Buonarrotti, and Raphael Sanzio—and the works they created. Nonfiction.

GENERAL WORKS ON THE RENAISSANCE:

Brooks, Polly Schoyer and Nancy Zinsser Walworth. *The World Awakes: The Renaissance in Western Europe*. New York: J.B. Lippincott Company, 1962. This is a good, old resource on the Renaissance from its beginnings in Italy to its spread to Spain, France, and England. Includes biographies of Lorenzo di Medici, Leonardo da Vinci, and William Shakespeare. Nonfiction.

Corrain, Lucia. *The Art of the Renaissance* (Masters of Art series). New York: Peter Bedrick Books, 1997. This is an engaging book that covers a very broad subject! You'll find entries on individual artists, cities, and techniques. Beautiful, full-color reproductions. Nonfiction.

Leon, Vicki. *Outrageous Women of the Renaissance*. New York: John Wiley & Sons. 1999. This book contains brief biographies written in a conversational style of women in world history. Unfortunately, you will not find anything about Sofonisba Anguissola in this collection. Nonfiction.

Matthews, Rupert. *Art and Civilization: The Renaissance* (Art and Civilization series). Lincolnwood, IL: NTC/Contemporary Publishing, 2000. This is a general source of artwork of the Renaissance with a good introduction and detailed captions. Nonfiction.

**KEY WORDS FOR RESEARCH ON
"ARTISTS OF THE ITALIAN RENAISSANCE"**

Sandro Botticelli, Filippo Brunelleschi, Florence, fresco, Leonardo da Vinci, humanism, Lorenzo di Medici, Michelangelo, Francesco Petrarch, Raphael, Renaissance, Sofonisba Anguissola

Acknowledgments

any people contributed their knowledge, talents, and enthusiasm to this book. We are indebted to a remarkable editorial staff, especially Heera Kang, and including Kristin Belsher, Allison Mangrum, and Patrice Gotsch. We also are indebted to Liliana Cartelli, the talented art director of the Explore the Ages series. She brought our ideas about pairing text and visuals to life and the result is more beautiful than we thought possible. We are grateful for helpful comments and suggestions on earlier drafts of this work by Dr. Diane L. Brooks, Dr. Cheryl A. Riggs, and David Vigilante. This book is dedicated to our fathers, Nicholas Stathis and Jerry Blanch, men who introduced us as children to the world of Renaissance art.

Gregory Blanch & Roberta Stathis

Dr. Blanch is on the faculty at New Mexico State University. Dr. Stathis is an educator, writer, and editor. They are co-authors of People and Stories in World History: A Historical Anthology *(Ballard & Tighe, 2003) and the other books in the Explore the Ages series—* Women Who Ruled, Leaders Who Changed the World, *and* Writers Who Inspired the World *(Ballard & Tighe, 2004).*